*This book is dedicated to all of my children, with a special mention to Imran, who has a fondness for the color red.*

# LITTLE RED'S JOURNEY
## to Saudi Arabia

*Independently Published by*
*Aysha Anastasia Izg*
*Muslim Joy*

*www.muslim-joy.com*

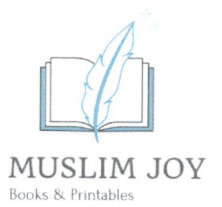

**MUSLIM JOY**
Books & Printables

*Copyright © 2024 by Aysha Anastasia Izg*
*All rights reserved. This book or any portion thereof*
*may not be reproduced or used in any manner whatsoever*
*without the express written permission of the publisher*
*except for the use of brief quotations in a book review.*
*Printed in the United States of America*

4

Greetings, young friends! I am Little Red, a curious and adventurous plane with big dreams of exploring the world.

Join me on an exciting adventure to the enchanting Land of Saudi Arabia.

What makes this land so special? Let me share with you.

Saudi Arabia is renowned for its two holiest sites, Makkah and Madinah.

6

Starting from my hometown Memphis, TN, I will embark on a journey flying through various cities and countries. Come along with me!

8

My journey began this morning as I departed Memphis and headed towards Washington DC, the capital of the United States.

10

Flying through Canada and even a part of Greenland, the longest stretch of my trip was over the vast Atlantic Ocean.

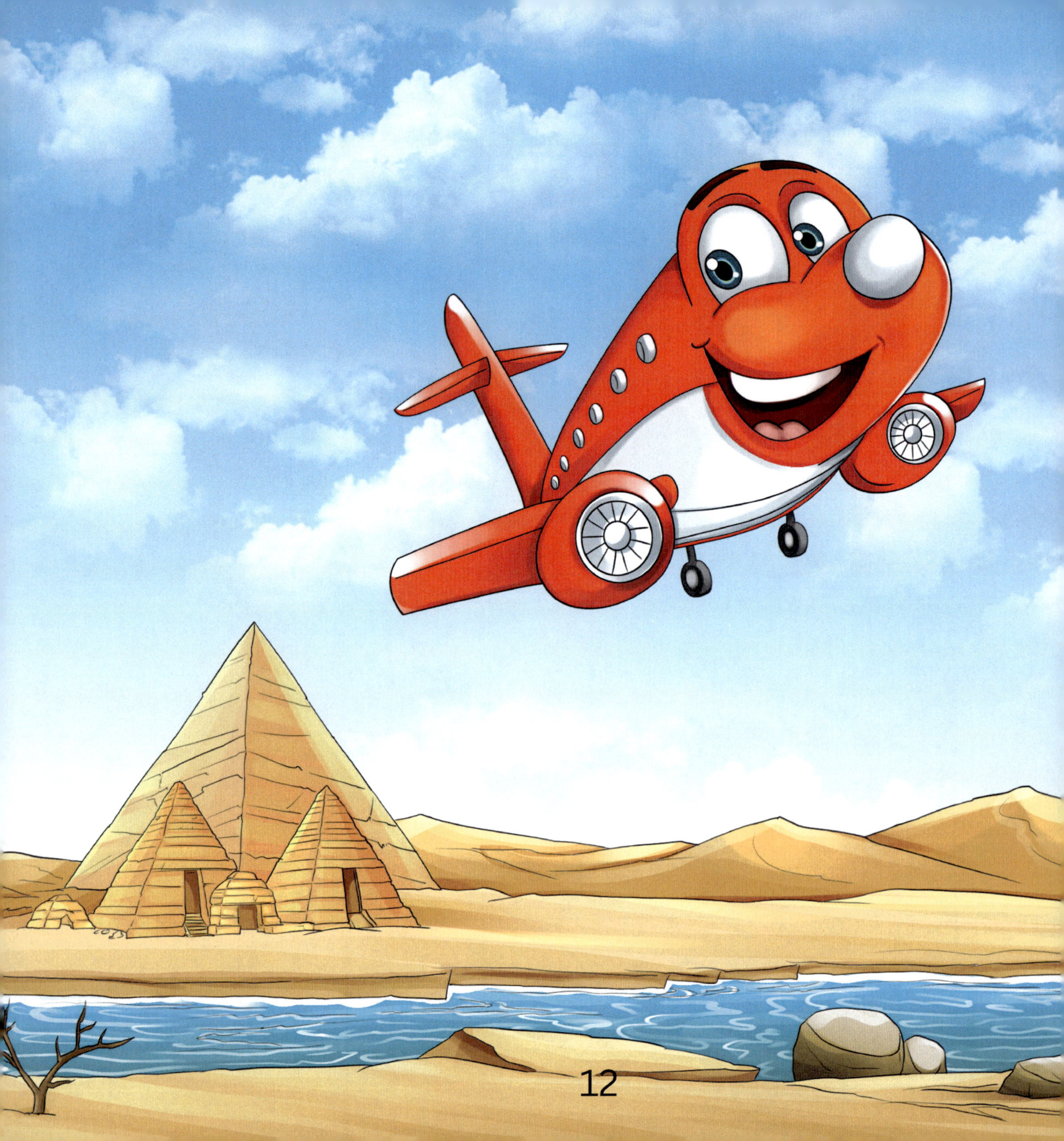

A brief stopover awaits me in Cairo, Egypt. Egypt, situated in Africa, is renowned for the Nile River, its longest river, and the ancient Pyramids. As I approach Egypt, I quickly fly over the Red Sea and head towards Madinah

14

Amidst the brightness, I wonder, what is this radiant city? It's the City of Light – could it be Madinah? Madinah al Munawarah, the other name for this city, welcomes me with its peaceful atmosphere and scorching noon heat of around 40°C at this time of year.

16

Admiring the magnificent minarets, I land near the Haram and observe a diverse crowd of people from various cultures conversing in different languages.

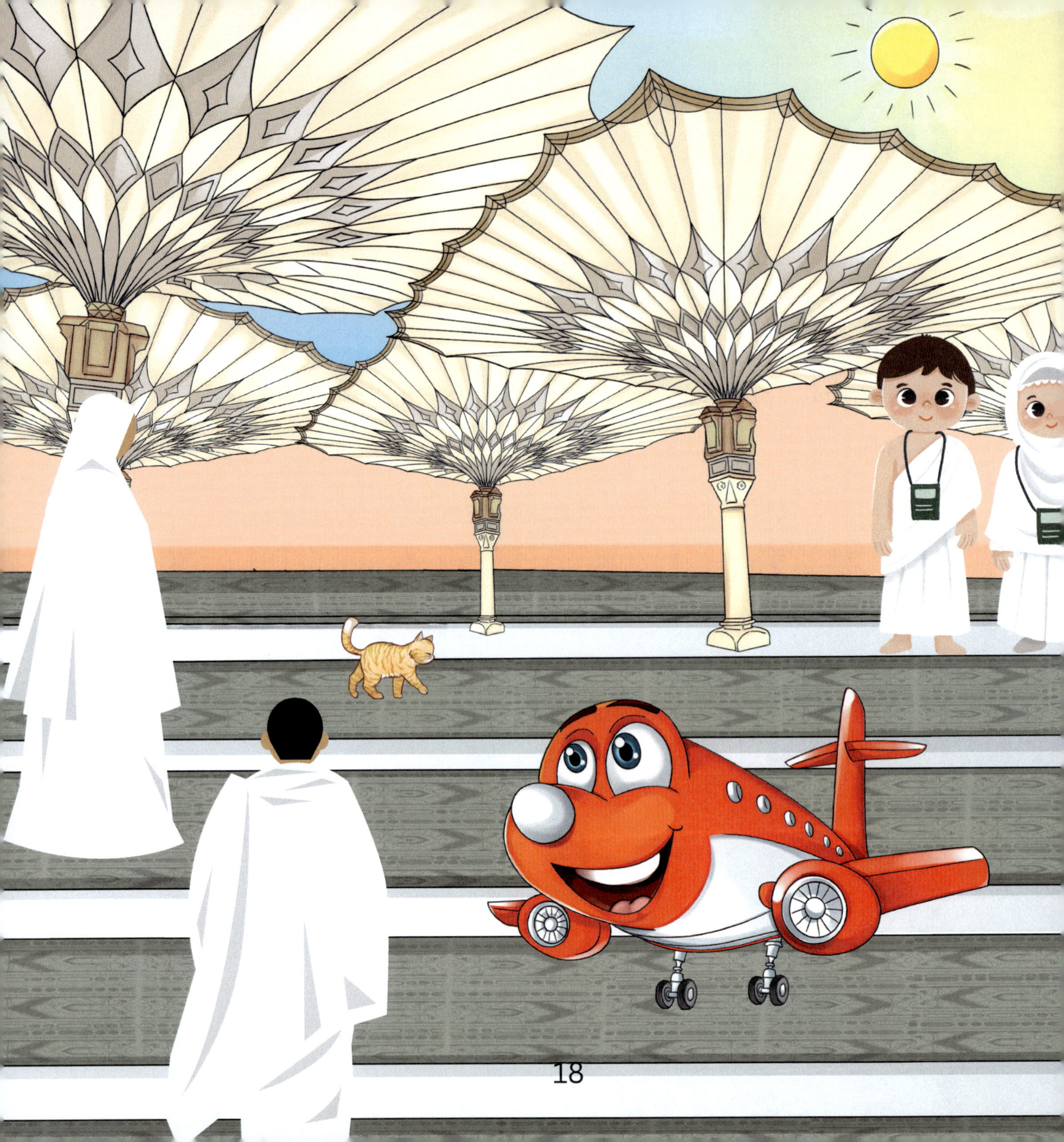

I am amazed by the melodious call to prayer and witness the grand umbrellas slowly unfurling to shield people from the blazing sun. While some choose to pray indoors, others pray under the mist and cool shelter of the umbrellas. The vast Masjid Nabawi can accommodate thousands of worshippers.

20

Leaving Masjid Nabawi, I venture to Masjid Quba, the first mosque in Madinah, and glide over Mount Uhud. These ancient mountains, some of which are volcanic, have stood for millennia, often unknown to many.

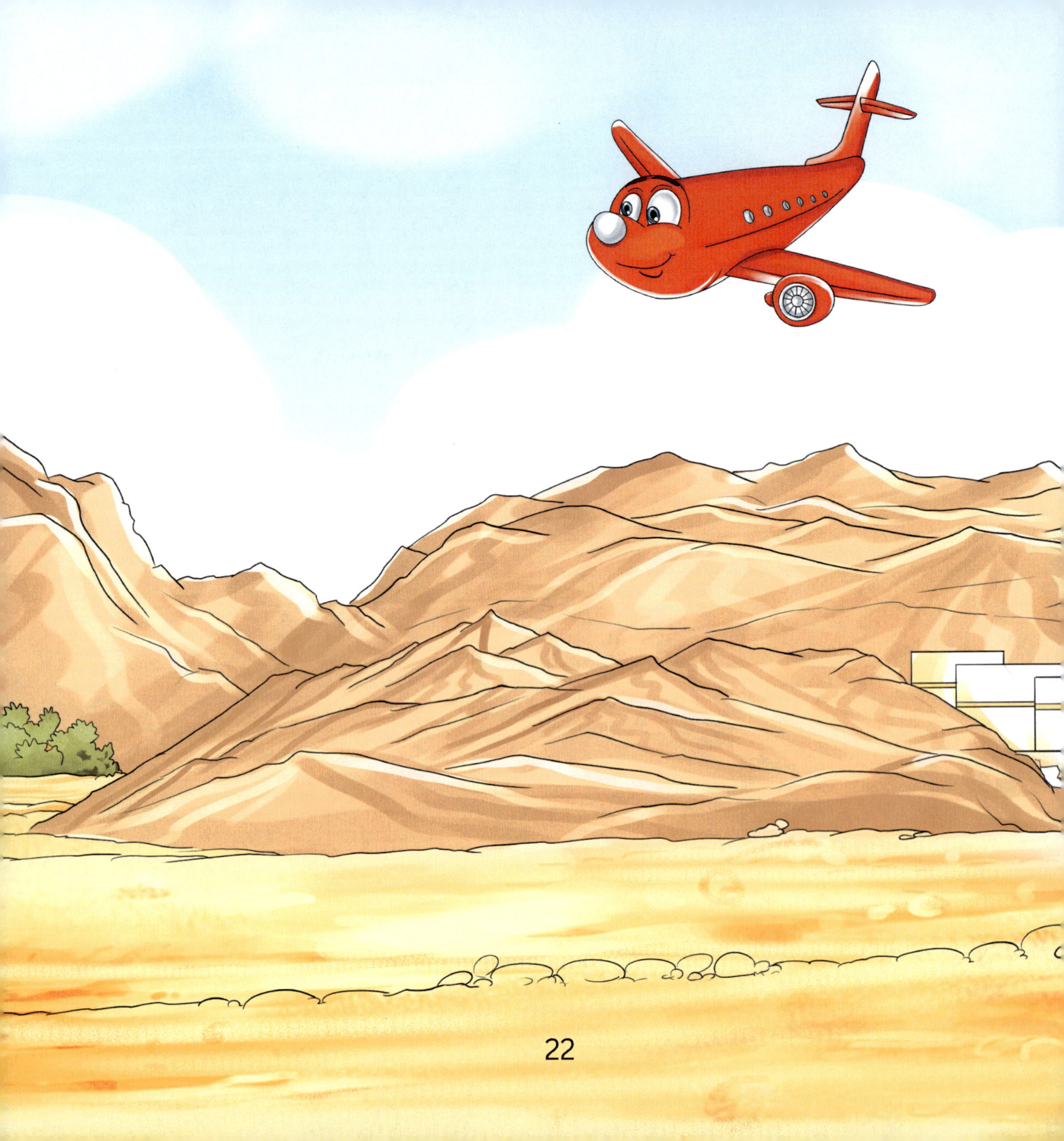

My journey continues to Makkah, soaring over mountains and desert hills until I spot a remarkable sight!

24

Oh what is it? Is that a bullet train? Indeed, it is the impressive Haramain bullet train, swiftly transporting passengers from Madinah to Makkah. As I fly by the train, I greet the passengers with a wave before landing near the Haram in Makkah.

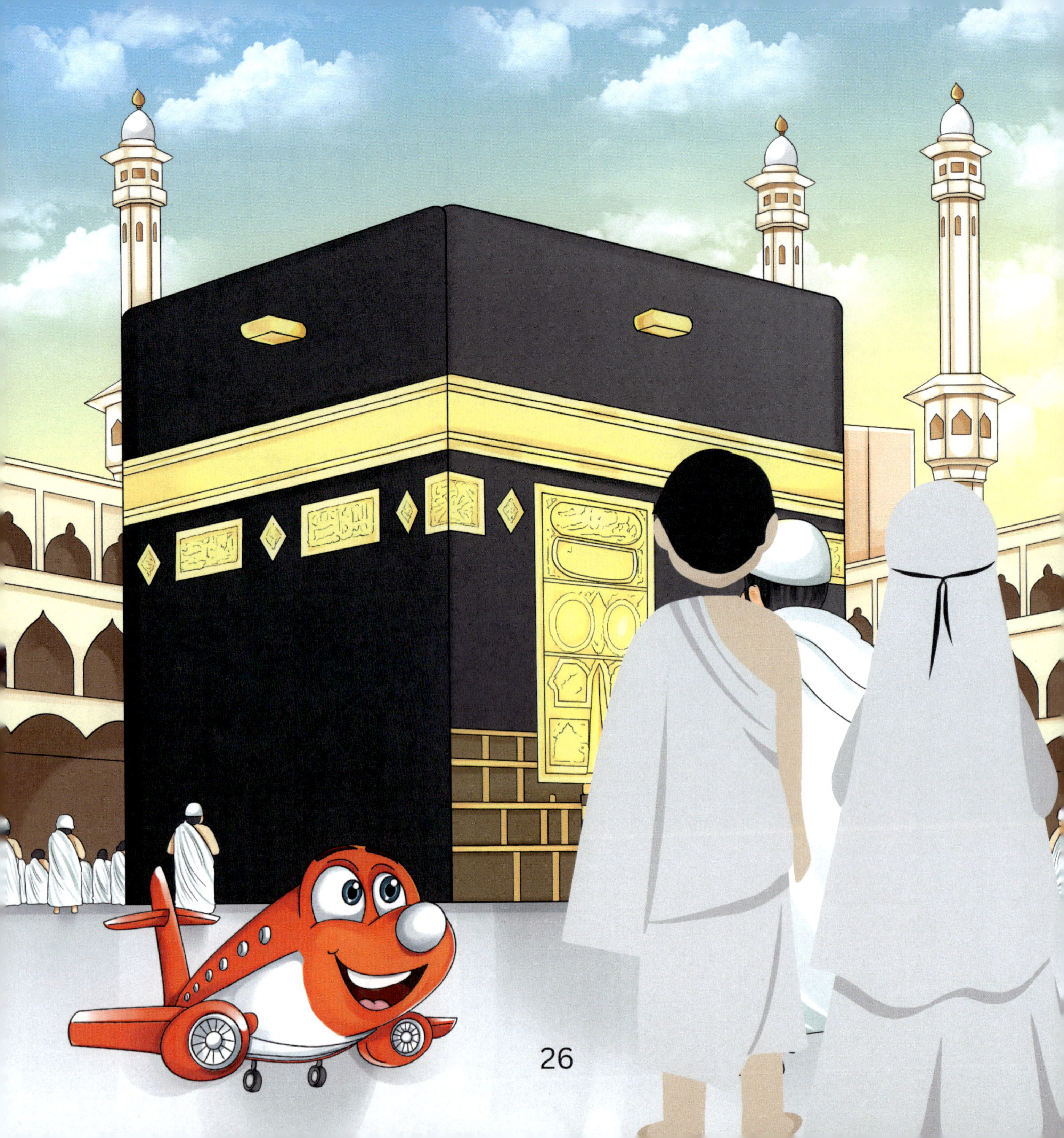

The area is crowded with even more people than in Madinah. Among the bustling crowd, worshipers walk in circles around the magnificent Kaaba, wearing white garments and performing their rituals.

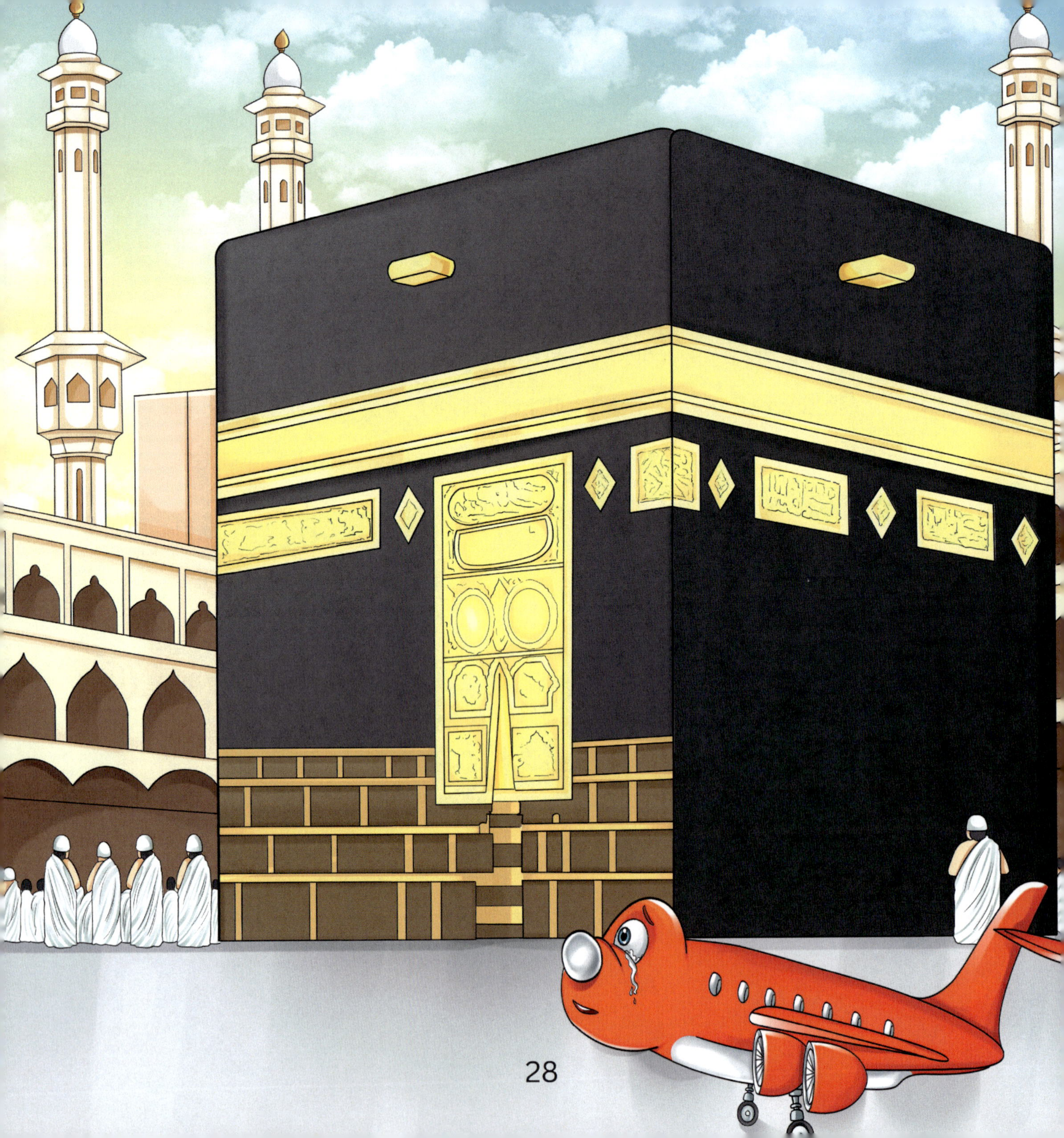

Overwhelmed with emotion, tears fall from my eyes as I see the Kaba for the first time ever. I make Dua from my heart for everyone in the world and then continue on my journey.

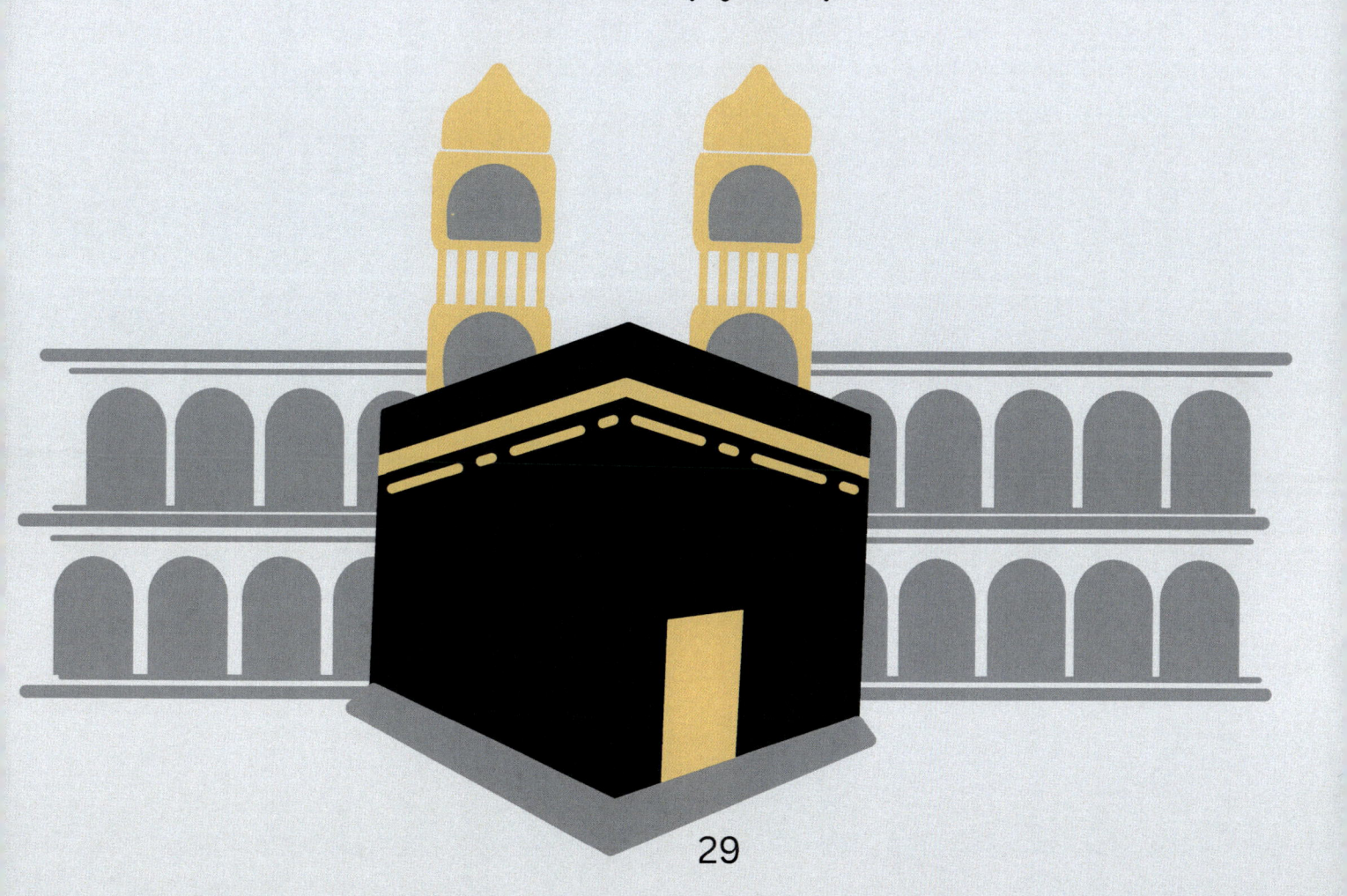

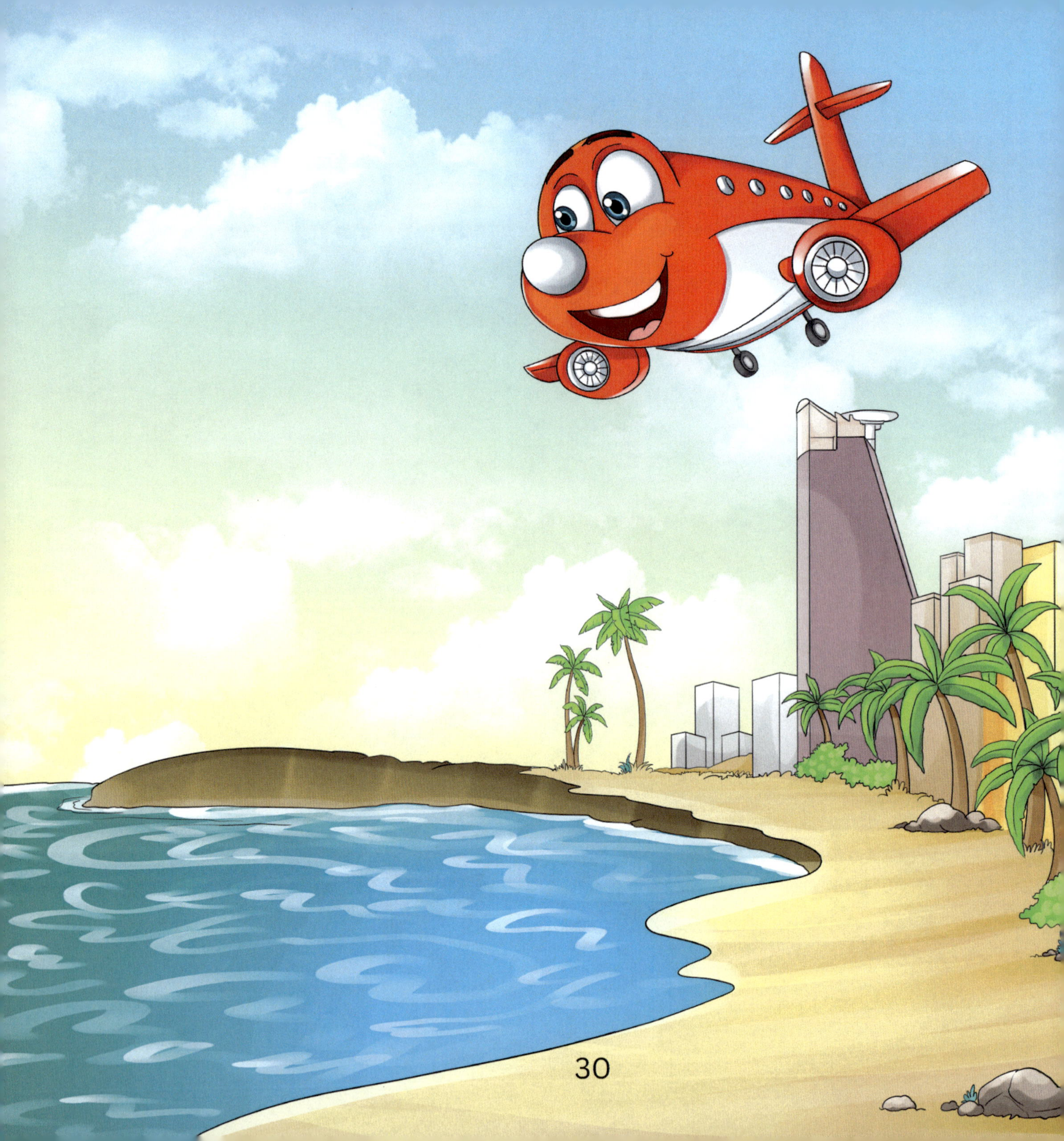

My final destination is Jeddah, a bustling city located on the Red Sea. The city's vastness and crowds left me in awe. During my visit, I marveled at the tallest fountain, explored the sea side, and admired the stunning aerial view of this beautiful city. Unexpectedly, I encountered a sandstorm that felt so much like a tornado.

Saudi Arabia has many more incredible places to explore, but now it's time for me to head back home. Stay tuned for my next exciting adventure!

Assalamu Aleikum

33

# Glossary

**The Kaaba,** is a stone building at the center of Islam's most important Mosque and Holiest site, the Masjid al-Haram (the sacred) in Mecca, Saudi Arabia. It is the qibla (direction of prayer) for Muslims around the world.
Muslims do not worship the Kaaba, but it is a sacred place of worship and holds great significance in Islam.

**Muslim's belief**: Muslims believe in one God (Allah), the angels, the prophets, the holy books, the Day of Judgment, and life after death.

**Masjid Nabawi**: al-Masjid an-Nabawī, also called the Prophet's Mosque, is a historic Mosque originally established and built by Prophet Muhammad (peace be upon him), situated in the city of Medina.

**Masjid Quba:** The Quba Mosque is a Mosque located in Medina, in the Hejaz region of Saudi Arabia, first built in the lifetime of Prophet Muhammad (peace be upon him) in the 7th century C.E. It is thought to be the first mosque in the world, established on the first day of Muhammad's (pbuh) emigration to Medina.

**Assalamu aleikum:** Islamic Greeting meaning "peace be to you".

**Al Munawarah**: The Enlightened City

Made in the USA
Middletown, DE
27 January 2025